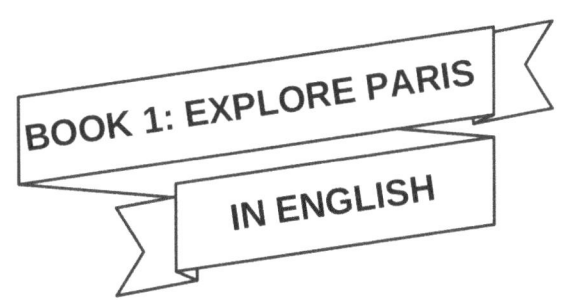

BOOK 1: EXPLORE PARIS

IN ENGLISH

Séverine Chanay-Savoyen

I dedicate this book to my incredible twins, Adalina and Kameli, and to their loving and generous uncle, Frédéric, whom I am proud to call my brother.

Published by Rainbows Publishing LLC
ISBN 13:9798989647439
Library of Congress Control Number: 2024909818

One sunny day, **Juliette** and **Julien** find a mysterious letter from their Uncle Fred in the mailbox! It is inviting them to **Paris** for an adventure.

What amazing things will they see?

They could visit the Eiffel Tower or 'la **Tour Eiffel**' as it is called in French, and perhaps enjoy tasty French treats.

The letter has a fancy seal and comes with two special **Adventure Passports**. "We are going to see so many cool places!" says Julien.

Are you ready to discover Paris with them?

Paris

DEPARTURE

PASSPORT

PAS

ADVENTURE awaits

N
W E
S

Juliette and Julien notice a beautiful symbol on the seal - it is called a **fleur-de-lis**!

This special flower symbol is very important in France. It has been used for many years, even by **kings**!

It used to be a sign for French kings. Did you know King Louis VII (Louis the 7th) was the very first one to use it?

What symbol would you choose if you were a king or queen? What makes it special to you?

Look at this big French map in Juliette and Julien's **book**! The country of **France** is located in Western Europe.

It has many neighbors like Germany, Italy, and Spain.

Can you find France on the big **map**? Its shape looks like a star!

Let's find Paris on the map of France! Did you know Paris is the capital **city** of France? It is right here, in the heart of the **country**.

"Oh, and look, Juliette! says Julien pointing at the map. France has two big oceans hugging its coast - the Atlantic Ocean on the left and the Mediterranean Sea to the South!"

Europe Continent

Where in the World

FRANCE

PARIS FRANCE

Atlantic Ocean

Germany

Italy

Spain

Mediterranean Sea

N E S W

love

In the book, they also see the French flag with its unique vertical blue, white, and red stripes.

In English, '**Bleu**' means blue, '**Blanc**' means white, and '**Rouge**' means red. These colors stand for main ideas: '**Bleu**' stands for freedom, '**Blanc**' stands for everyone being equal, and '**Rouge**' stands for friends working together.

The French **flag** and its colors became powerful symbols during the French Revolution. On July 14, 1789, an event known as the Storming of the Bastille helped free the French people from the king's bullying.

French people around the world celebrate **Bastille Day** every year to remember these important ideas.

Find the French flag on the coloring page and use your blue and red crayons to color the stipes.

When Juliette and Julien arrive in Paris, they meet Uncle Fred at the '**Gare du Nord**,' which is the North Station **train**.

With open arms, he greets them with '**Bienvenue** à Paris!' and '**Bonjour**!', which in French means 'Welcome!' and 'Hello!'.

Juliette and Julien love sharing words in French with you! Do you agree that learning to say things in another language is so much fun?

If you were in Paris, how would you say hello to someone? What fun French greeting would you choose?

Juliette and Julien learn a new French expression from Uncle Fred: **'joie de vivre'**. It means 'joy of living'.

In France, this is a special way of enjoying life with happiness and enthusiasm.

It is about loving good food, **beautiful** art, and spending time with **friends**. The French really know how to find joy in little things.

What makes you feel like 'joie de vivre' in your life?

Juliette and Julien admire the tall **Eiffel Tower** and learn that Gustave Eiffel constructed it specifically for a big fair in 1889.

It was built to celebrate 100 years since an important event called the French Revolution. The tower was so different and new that not everyone liked it at first, but now it is a **famous** monument in Paris.

As they arrive at the Eiffel Tower, Juliette and Julien start their climb up the stairs, counting each step in French as they go: '**Un**, **deux**, **trois**, **quatre**, **cinq**, **six**, **sept**, **huit**, **neuf** and **dix**'!

From the top, Paris looks tiny and beautiful. *How high can you count in French?*

Inside the big **Louvre Museum**, Juliette and Julien are amazed by many paintings, especially the **Mona Lisa**, which was painted by Leonardo da Vinci.

'**Peinture**' means painting in French.

Mona Lisa's smile is mysterious, and her eyes seem to follow you everywhere!

They wonder about Mona Lisa's secret thoughts.

Can you guess what she might be thinking?

Inside **Notre Dame Cathedral**, Juliette and Julien admire the Gothic architecture. The cathedral was built long, long ago around 1345 and is located on a **small** island in the middle of the **Seine River**.

They search for mythical creatures and gargoyles. 'Look at that gargoyle!' exclaims Juliette.

These spooky statues, designed in the Gothic style with sharp arches and big **windows**, were believed to protect the cathedral.

Juliette wonders if these creatures are real, or part of old legends. In French, '**Légende**' means legend.

Legends are old **stories** about brave heroes and magical creatures that people have told for a long time.

Notre Dame

LÉGENDE

Juliette and Julien find artists painting vibrant scenes in colorful Montmartre. "Look at all these **colors**!" Juliette says.

They learn '**vert**' for the color of grass, '**orange**' for the fruit, '**jaune**' for the sun, '**noir**' for the night sky, '**gris**' for rainy clouds, '**violet**' like flowers, and '**marron**' like chocolate."

What would you paint using these beautiful French colors?

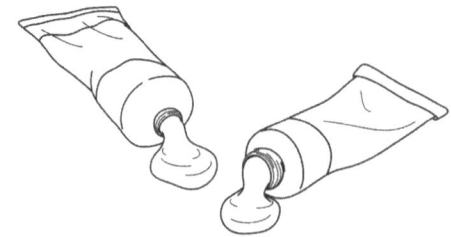

In Montmartre, Juliette and Julien taste **crêpes.** These are thin pancakes that are often filled with sweet like **sugar** or salty fillings like **ham** and '**fromage**' which means cheese in French.

As they learn about '**vert**', '**rose**', '**jaune**', and other French colors, they enjoy the tasty treat.

"What color is your crêpe?" Juliette giggles, comparing it to their color palette.

After their adventures, Juliette and Julien relax at a charming **pâtisserie** - a special shop for French pastries- different from a **boulangerie** that mainly sells **bread**.

While drinking warm chocolate milk, they gaze at a display of sweets. They see **éclairs**, light and creamy, and **macarons**, small and colorful with a sweet crunch.

"Look, that is a **tarte** and a **gâteau**!" Julien says, sharing new words for pie and cake with you.

"So many delicious choices!" Juliette smiles.

Which delightful French treat catches your eye in the patisserie?

In the patisserie, Juliette and Julien learn about **'goûter**,' the French snack time that kids love. Goûter is when children enjoy treats like **madeleines** after school.

Madeleines are small shell-shaped butter cakes. These treats became popular around the Second World War. Madeleines are special because they need a unique baking pan to get their shape.

"These madeleines are perfect for goûter!" says Julien.

Would you like to try making these for your snack time?

Scan the QR code for an easy way **to bake** madeleines and see how French kids enjoy their goûter. Do not forget, you need an adult to help you with the recipe.

Classic French Madeleines

SCAN ME

Ingredients

- 3/4 cup all-purpose flour
- 1 1/2 tsp baking powder
- a pinch of salt
- 1 squeeze of lemon juice
- 7 tbsp unsalted butter
- 1/2 cup white sugar
- 2 large eggs
- 1 tbsp honey

♡ Instructions ♡

In a large bowl, slowly whisk eggs and sugar for 1 minute, then add honey and whisk for 3 more minutes until foamy.

Melt butter in a saucepan, add a squeeze of lemon juice and pinch of salt, then cool.

Sift flour and baking powder into the egg mix, whisk until smooth.

Add cooled butter, whisk to a smooth batter, and rest for 2 hours at room temperature.

Butter a madeleine pan, fill each mold with a generous spoon of batter.

Bake at 425 °F for 3 minutes, then reduce to 390 °F and bake for another 6-7 minutes.

Cool the madeleines briefly, then remove from the mold and enjoy warm.

Cooking time: 10 min

BUTTER

FLOUR

SUGAR

HONEY

Juliette and Julien are amazed at the "**Arc de Triomphe,"** standing tall at the end of the famous "**Champs-Élysées**."

"It is like a huge, tall gateway!" says Juliette. The Champs-Élysées is known for its beautiful, long avenue, leading right to this monument.

This arch-building honors soldiers who fought for France, especially during the wars led by Napoleon. '**Triomphe**' is a French word that means 'winning' or 'doing really well at something. It is like when you win a game or do something great!

How would you celebrate a big achievement, like winning a game or doing something amazing? What would you do to celebrate?

As Juliette and Julien prepare to say goodbye to Paris, they reflect on all the wonderful places they have seen and the new treats they tasted.

They look at their **souvenirs**, each a small piece of their Paris adventure. "We will always remember our time in Paris," Juliette smiles. "And all the amazing things we discovered!" adds Julien.

As they wave **au revoir** to Paris, the City of Light, also known as **La Ville Lumière**, they know that these memories will stay with them forever.

Have you learned new French words and tasted delicious treats like **éclairs** and **gâteaux**? *What was your favorite part of exploring Paris?*

English	French	Pronounciation	Page
Juliette	Juliette	zhoo-lee-ET	
Julien	Julien	zhoo-LYEN	
Paris	Paris	pah-REE	**1**
Passport	Passeport	pahs-por	
Adventure	Aventure	ah-vahn-TUR	
Eiffel Tower	Tour Eiffel	toor ey-FEHL	
Lily Flower	Fleur de Lis	flur duh LEES	**3**
Kings	Rois	rwah	
Book	Livre	lee-vruh	
France	France	frahns	
Map	Carte	kart	**5**
City	Ville	veel	
Country	Pays	pay-ee	
Flag	Drapeau	dra-poh	
Bastille Day	La Fête Nationale	lah fet nah-syon-al	**7**
White	Blanc	blahn	
Blue	Bleu	bluh	
Red	Rouge	roozh	

English	French	Pronounciation	Page
North Station	Gare du Nord	gahr duh nohr	
Train	Train	trahn	
Welcome	Bienvenue	byan-ven-ew	**9**
Hello!	Bonjour!	bon-zhoor!	
Good evening	Bonsoir	bohn-swahr	
Hi!	Salut!	sah-lew!	**10**
How are you?	Comment ça va?	koh-mah sah vah?	
What's up?	Ça va?	sah vah?	
Good afternoon	Bonne après-midi	bon ah-preh mee-dee	
Good night	Bonne nuit	bon nwee	
Joy of living	Joie de vivre	zhwa duh veev	
Beautiful	Beau(m) / Belle(f)	boh(m) / bell(f)	**11**
Friend	Ami(m) / Amie(f)	ah-mee(m) (f)	
Eiffel Tower	Tour Eiffel	tour-eh-FEHL	
Famous	Célèbre	seh-leb-ruh	
Zero	Zéro	zay-roh	
One	Un	uhN	**13**
Two	Deux	duh	
Three	Trois	trwah	

English	French	Pronounciation	Page
Four	Quatre	kah-truh	
Five	Cinq	sank	
Six	Six	seess	**13**
Seven	Sept	sept	
Eight	Huit	wheat	
Nine	Neuf	nuhf	
Ten	Dix	deess	
Louvre	Louvre	loo-vruh	
Museum	Musée	mew-zay	**15**
Mona Lisa	La Joconde	lah zhoh-kond	
Painting	Peinture	pan-TUR	**16**
Blue	Bleu	bluh	
Red	Rouge	roo-zhuh	
Notre Dame	Notre-Dame	noh-truh dahm	
Windows	Fenêtres	fuh-nehtr	
Legend	Légende	lay-ZHAWND	**17**
Small	Petit(m) / Petite(f)	peh-tee(m)/peh-teet(f)	
Stories	Histoires	ees-twar	
The Seine River	La Seine	lah sen	

34

English	French	Pronounciation	Page
Colors	Couleurs	koo-luhr	
Blue	Bleu	bluh	
White	Blanc	blahn	
Red	Rouge	roo-zhuh	
Green	Vert	vair	
Orange	Orange	oh-RAHN-zhuh	19
Yellow	Jaune	zhohn	
Black	Noir	nwahr	
Gray	Gris	gree	
Violet	Violet	vee-oh-LEH	
Brown	Marron	mah-ROHN	
Crepes	Crêpes	krep	
Sugar	Sucre	suh-kruh	
Ham	Jambon	zhan-bohn	
Cheese	Fromage	froh-MAHzhuh	21
Green	Vert	vair	
Rose	Rose	rohz	
Yellow	Jaune	zhohn	

English	French	Pronounciation	Page
Pastry shop	Pâtisserie	pah-tee-suh-REE	
Bakery	Boulangerie	boo-lahn-zhuh-REE	
Bread	Pain	pan	
Eclairs	Éclairs	ay-KLEHR	**23**
Macarons	Macarons	mah-kah-ROHN	
Tart	Tarte	tahrt	
Cake	Gâteau	gah-toh	**24**
Croissant	Croissant	krwah-sahn	
French Napoleon	Mille-feuille	meel-foy	
Profiteroles	Profiteroles	proh-fee-teh-rohl	
Cream puff	Chou	shoo	
Snack	Goûter	goo-TAY	
Madeleines	Madeleines	mah-duh-layn	**25**
To bake	Cuire	kweer	
Arc de Triomphe	Arc de Triomphe	ark duh tree-ohmf	
Champs-Élysées	Champs-Élysées	shahntz-ay-lee-zay	**27**
Triumph	Triomphe	tree-ohm-fuh	

English	French	Pronounciation	Page
Souvenirs	Souvenirs	soo-vuh-neer	
Goodbye	Au revoir	oh ruh-vwahr	29
Eclairs	Éclairs	ay-KLEHR	
Cake	Gâteau	gah-toh	
City of Lights	La Ville Lumière	lah veel lum-mee-AIR	

Disclaimers

Please remember that the way people talk can be different in different places. This means some words might sound different or have different meanings depending on where you live or come from.

The QR code takes you to a website we do not control. Please let us know if the link stops working.

 # The Series

Explore Paris
Spanish Edition
Book 1
Available Now!

Christmas at
the North Pole
Book 1 – coming
Fall 2024

Explore
The Theater
Book 1
Available Now!

Christmas Around
the World
Book 1 – coming
Fall 2024

Explore India
Book 1 – coming
Fall 2024

Explore
New York City
Book 2– coming
Fall 2024

Made in the USA
Lake Mary, FL
30 March 2024